THE PERSON BEHIND THE BRAND

BOBBI BROWN

WRITTEN BY ANNETTE WHIPPLE

ILLUSTRATED BY GARY BOLLER

TABLE OF CONTENTS

A Starfish Book

SEAHORSE PUBLISHING

Teaching Tips for Caregivers:

As a caregiver, you can help your child succeed in school by giving them a strong foundation in language and literacy skills and a desire to learn to read.

This book helps children grow by letting them practice reading skills.

Reading for pleasure and interest will help your child develop reading skills and will give your child the opportunity to practice these skills in meaningful ways.

- Encourage your child to read on their own at home.
- Encourage your child to practice reading aloud.
- Encourage activities that require reading.
- Establish a reading time.
- Talk with your child.
- Give your child writing materials.

Teaching Tips for Teachers:

Research shows that one of the best ways for students to learn a new topic is to read about it.

Before Reading

- Read the "Words to Know" and discuss the meaning of each word.
- Read the back cover to see what the book is about.

During Reading

- When a student gets to a word that is unknown, ask them to look at the rest of the sentence to find clues to help with the meaning of the unknown word.
- Ask the student to write down any pages of the book that were confusing to them.

After Reading

- Discuss the main idea of the book.
- Ask students to give one detail that they learned from the book by showing a text-dependent answer from the book.

BOBBI BROWN—BOBBI BROWN COSMETICS

Young Bobbi Brown liked to watch her mom put on **makeup**.

One day, she would change how people wore makeup.

Bobbi was born in 1957.

She grew up in Chicago, Illinois.

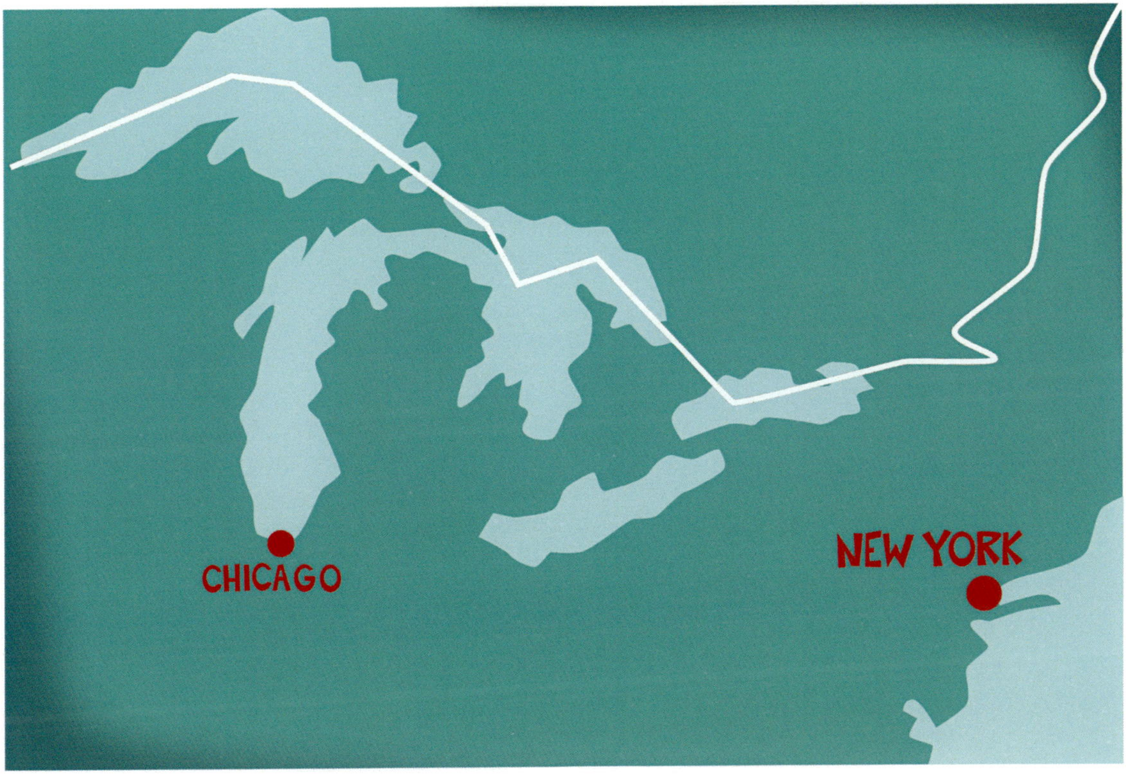

Bobbi loved to try different kinds of makeup.

She went to college to learn more about **cosmetics**. After college, she moved to New York City.

Bobbi became a makeup artist.

She used **lipstick**, powder, and more to change how people looked.

Bobbi worked with many photographers and **models**.

Bobbi thought that people should look **natural**.

She did not like makeup that was too bold and bright.

Bobbi mixed and blended makeup.

Then, it did not look fake.

Bobbi wanted to help people be healthy and happy.

She wanted them to look good and feel good.

Bobbi said, “Your natural face is your most beautiful face.”

Bobbi met a scientist who could create new kinds of makeup.

She told the scientist what colors she wanted.

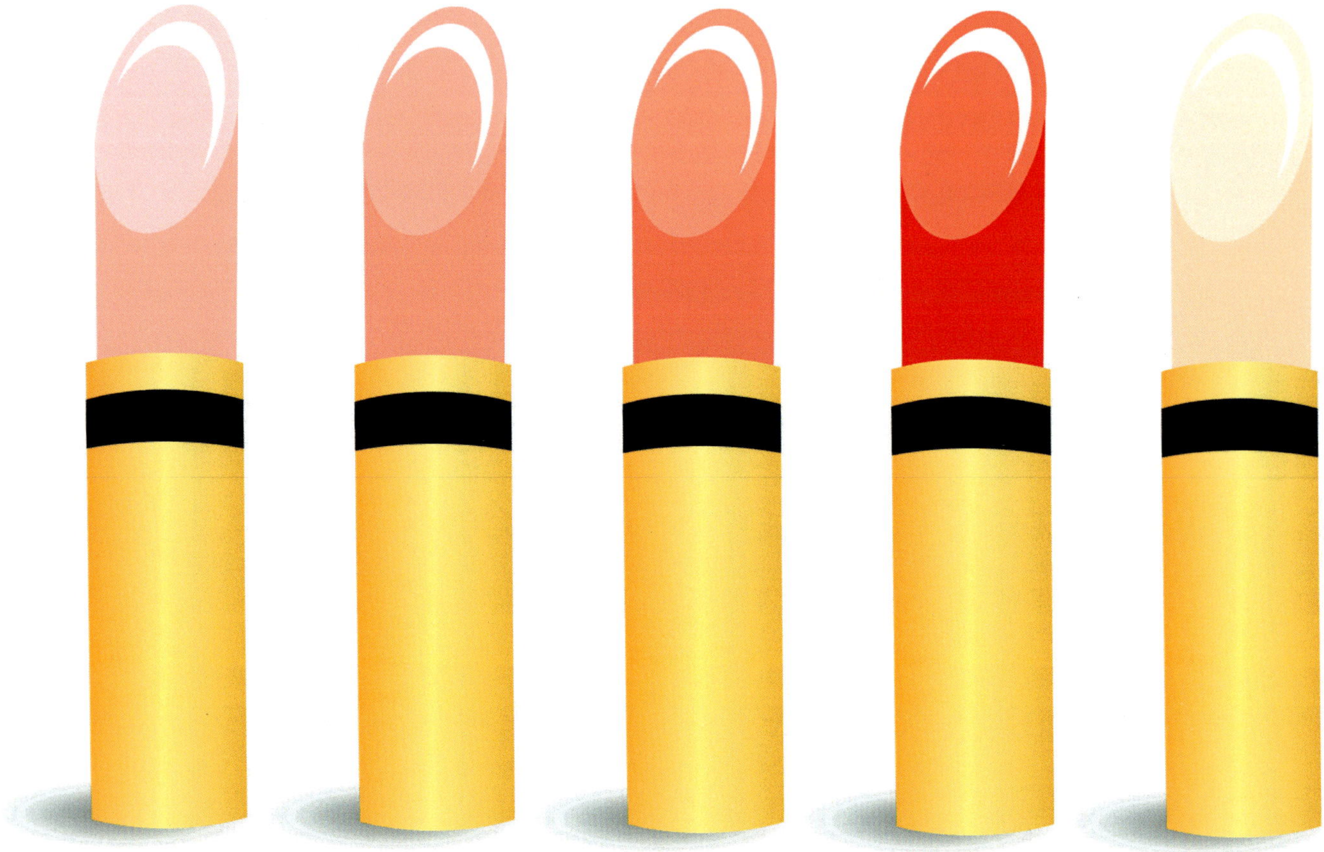

Bobbi and the scientist created
a pinkish-brown lipstick.

It looked natural.

They made nine more colors.

Bobbi was in **business**!

She started the Bobbi Brown Cosmetics company.

BOBBI BROWN

Many people ordered from Bobbi.

They loved makeup that looked natural.

Bobbi's business grew.

BOBBI BROWN
BOBBI BROWN

Over time, Bobbi's company tried new things.

They made different kinds of cosmetics.

BOBBI BROWN

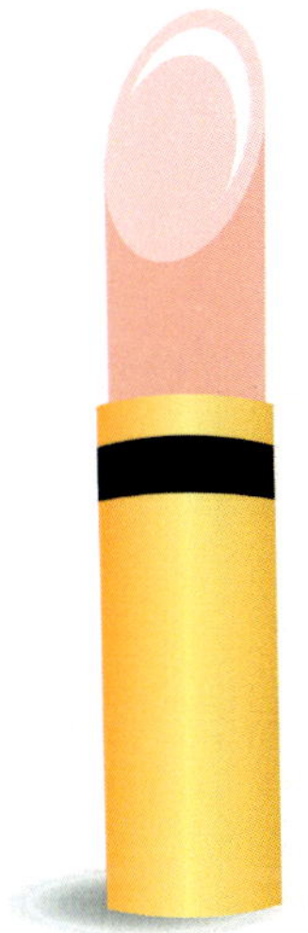

in 2014

Bobbi still creates makeup.

She still helps people look natural and beautiful.

WORDS TO KNOW

business (BIZ-nis): activity related to selling things

cosmetics (kahz-MET-iks): beauty products

lipstick (LIP-stik): a crayon-like product used to color lips

makeup (MAKE-up): products put on the face to change how it looks

models (MAH-duhlz): people who have their pictures taken to help sell products such as clothes and makeup

natural (NACH-ur-uhl): normal, relaxed, and unchanged; not pretending

INDEX

COMPREHENSION QUESTIONS

1. Bobbi Brown grew up in the city of ______ .

a. Atlanta

b. Philadelphia

c. Chicago

2. Bobbi began her business with 10 different colors of ______ .

a. powder

b. lipstick

c. blush

3. Bobbi's makeup focuses on ______ .

a. bright colors

b. bold colors

c. natural beauty

4. True or false: Bobbi wanted to help people feel beautiful.

5. True or false: Bobbi worked with a photographer to create natural-looking makeup.

Answers:
1. c, 2. b, 3. c, 4. True, 5. False

ABOUT THE AUTHOR

Annette Whipple celebrates curiosity through her books. She wrote *The Laura Ingalls Wilder Companion*, *Whooo Knew? The Truth About Owls*, and *Quirky Critter Devotions*. She lives with her family in Pennsylvania where she appreciates the natural beauty around her. Get to know Annette at www.AnnetteWhipple.com.

ABOUT THE ILLUSTRATOR

Gary Boller lives in the glorious countryside in Hampshire, UK, with his wife and two children, one Chihuahua, and four cats. He always doodled as a kid, even on his parents' walls, and loved the comics of the day. Gary also loves music and has played double bass in bands. He has toured all over Europe many times and the USA twice. He's currently learning fiddle, much to the annoyance of his pets.

Written by: Annette Whipple
Illustrated by: Gary Boller
Designed by: Under the Oaks
Editor: Kim Thompson

Library of Congress PCN Data
Bobbi Brown / Annette Whipple
The Person Behind the Brand
ISBN 979-8-8945-9115-5 (hard cover)
ISBN 979-8-8945-9120-9 (paperback)
ISBN 979-8-8945-9130-8 (EPUB)
ISBN 979-8-8945-9125-4 (eBook)
Library of Congress Control Number: 2024946240

Printed in Canada/012025/CP20250101

Seahorse Publishing Company
www.seahorsepub.com

Published in the United States
Seahorse Publishing
PO Box 771325
Coral Springs, FL 33077

SEAHORSE PUBLISHING